Dogs on Duty
Herding Dogs

by Marie Brandle

Bullfrog Books

Ideas for Parents and Teachers

Bullfrog Books let children practice reading informational text at the earliest reading levels. Repetition, familiar words, and photo labels support early readers.

Before Reading

- Discuss the cover photo. What does it tell them?

- Look at the picture glossary together. Read and discuss the words.

Read the Book

- "Walk" through the book and look at the photos. Let the child ask questions. Point out the photo labels.

- Read the book to the child, or have him or her read independently.

After Reading

- Prompt the child to think more. Ask: Did you know about herding dogs before reading this book? What more would you like to learn about them?

Bullfrog Books are published by Jump!
5357 Penn Avenue South
Minneapolis, MN 55419
www.jumplibrary.com

Copyright © 2022 Jump! International copyright reserved in all countries. No part of this book may be reproduced in any form without written permission from the publisher.

Library of Congress Cataloging-in-Publication Data

Names: Brandle, Marie, 1989– author.
Title: Herding dogs / Marie Brandle.
Description: Minneapolis: Jump!, Inc., 2022.
Series: Dogs on duty | Includes index.
Audience: Ages 5–8
Identifiers: LCCN 2021017902 (print)
LCCN 2021017903 (ebook)
ISBN 9781645279259 (hardcover)
ISBN 9781645279266 (paperback)
ISBN 9781645279273 (ebook)
Subjects: LCSH: Herding dogs—Juvenile literature.
Classification: LCC SF428.6 .B73 2022 (print)
LCC SF428.6 .B73 2022 (ebook) | DDC 636.737—dc23
LC record available at https://lccn.loc.gov/2021017902
LC ebook record available at https://lccn.loc.gov/2021017903

Editor: Eliza Leahy
Designer: Molly Ballanger

Photo Credits: Maja H./Shutterstock, cover (dog); Budimir Jevtic/Shutterstock, cover (sheep); Erik Lam/Shutterstock, 1; Eric Isselee/Shutterstock, 3, 24; Anne Richard/Shutterstock, 4, 20–21; Darlene Cutshall/Shutterstock, 5, 23bl; tkyszk/Shutterstock, 6–7; Grant Faint/Getty, 8–9, 23tl, 23tr; ms.yenes/Shutterstock, 10; Elton Abreu/Shutterstock, 11, 12–13, 23br; Shutterstock, 14–15, 16; Phil Silverman/Shutterstock, 17; Pete Oxford/Minden Pictures/SuperStock, 18–19; AngelaMedler/iStock, 22tl; michelangeloop/Shutterstock, 22tm; Sally Wallis/Shutterstock, 22tr; daseaford/Shutterstock, 22bl; Marcelino Pozo Ruiz/Shutterstock, 22bm; Danny Ye/Shutterstock, 22br.

Printed in the United States of America at Corporate Graphics in North Mankato, Minnesota.

Table of Contents

On the Farm

This is a herding dog!

Her job is to herd farm animals.

She runs in circles around them.

She moves sheep from one field to another.

They find more grass to eat.

field

handler

The dog's owner
is a handler.

He gives commands.

They work together!

This herding dog barks.

Then he runs at the cows.

The cows move in one direction.

Oh, no! There is a stray.
The dog herds her, too.
Staying together
keeps the cows safe.

Dogs herd many farm animals.

This dog herds goats.

He leads them.

This dog herds chickens.

This one herds ducks!

Some herding dogs work together.

It is almost dark.

The dog herds sheep into the barn.

They stay safe there!

On the Job

Herding dogs herd many kinds of farm animals.
Take a look at some of them!

chickens

cows

ducks

geese

goats

sheep

Picture Glossary

commands
Orders that are given.

handler
A person who trains or controls an animal.

herd
To move animals in a group.

stray
An animal that is separated from its group.

Index

To Learn More

Finding more information is as easy as 1, 2, 3.

❶ Go to www.factsurfer.com

❷ Enter "herdingdogs" into the search box.

❸ Choose your book to see a list of websites.